HISTORICAL MAP

OF

PENNSYLVANIA.

SHOWING THE

INDIAN NAMES OF STREAMS, AND VILLAGES, AND
PATHS OF TRAVEL;

THE SITES OF OLD FORTS AND BATTLE-FIELDS;

THE SUCCESSIVE PURCHASES FROM THE INDIANS; AND THE
NAMES AND DATES OF COUNTIES AND COUNTY TOWNS;

WITH

TABLES OF FORTS AND PROPRIETARY MANORS

EDITED BY

P. W. SHEAFER
AND OTHERS

PUBLICATION FUND
OF THE
HISTORICAL SOCIETY OF PENNSYLVANIA,
820 Spruce Street, Philadelphia
1875

Entered according to Act of Congress, in the year 1875, by
THE TRUSTEES OF THE PUBLICATION FUND OF THE HISTORICAL
SOCIETY OF PENNSYLVANIA,
in the Office of the Librarian of Congress, at Washington

COLLINS PRINTER

HISTORICAL MAP OF PENNSYLVANIA.

The aboriginal nomenclature of Pennsylvania has been frequently commended for its beauty and appropriateness. The Indian dialect spoken here was soft and liquid, and unusually free from the guttural sounds characteristic of the language elsewhere. Lackawanna, Susquehanna, Juniata, Monongahela are names which for euphony are rarely equalled. The tendency of our people to change the Indian names—and the mispronunciation which is often equivalent to an entire change—are fast obliterating these original designations. Callapatscink is now known as the Yellow Breeches, Whopehawly as Wapwallopen, and the beautiful little stream called the Pema Pecha is corrupted into Pennypack.

To arrest these changes, or at least to note them, is essential both as a matter of history, and a matter of geography.

A map, while it seems only to display an existing condition, may, however—and most truly—be called a herald of the approaching future. Who, for instance, can look upon the admirable work of Nicholas Scull, of 1759, with the various Indian Paths crossing the territory, and the chain of forts stretching along the advancing frontier, without clearly perceiving that two races were coming into hostile contact, and that in future years the conflict for superiority must ensue. That era has passed away, and with victory achieved by the civilized man, the plough has obliterated the mound over the remains of the fallen warrior, while the graver's tool leaves on newer maps no trace of fort, or path, or Indian village. Like the Swedish names on Lindstrom's map—produced more than a century earlier than Scull's—they have been swept away by the tide of mighty progress which has left but a portion of their débris in libraries, those quiet eddies of the flood.

Thoughts like these would seem to have moved the late Mr. J. Francis Fisher to offer, at a meeting of the Historical Society, his resolutions of the 12th of December, 1853, for the appointment of a committee to collect and prepare material for the restoration of Indian names, and, subsequently, a fellow-member, Mr. Peter W Sheafer, of Pottsville, to undertake the preparation of an historical map of Pennsylvania. The latter work—commenced without a previous knowledge of Mr. Fisher's proposal—has since had incorporated with it the information that resulted from that earlier effort. In the spring of 1873, this map was thought to be in a fit condition to be engraved, so that impressions might be sent to gentlemen in every part of the State, with a request that they would make such additions as might be within their power. This has been done, and with the admirable results now included. The map, with much that is valuable, but with topographical defects best appreciated by those who have prepared it, will ensure, it is hoped, acquisitions of historical and geographical information from aged surveyors and others whose knowledge, if not thus obtained, must soon be buried with themselves.

The tables of historical events, of manors, and of forts, may serve, it is hoped, to indicate the direction in which it is desirable that investigation should be made.

The maps of Pennsylvania, not being the results of actual connected surveys, are so defective and inaccurate as to render an exact location a matter of great difficulty. The geologist cannot satisfactorily exhibit the results of his examinations, nor can the student of history trace the movements of man—the courses, for instance, of the Indians through the mountain gaps, when, during the long years of the French and Indian War, they devastated so large a portion of Pennsylvania.

The enormous expenditure likely to be incurred in the production of a correct map of the whole State, might be avoided, were the Legislature to authorize the ascertainment of the different county lines, which are variously laid down on different maps, and the plotting from the manuscripts retained in their various offices, of the surveys of the numerous railroads and canals This would result in securing, at the cost of but a few thousand dollars, correct outlines and boundaries, as well as a vast amount of correct topography, for which latter there has been expended by the companies, in their surveys, sums of money amounting to perhaps quite one and a half million dollars. Should the Legislature do this, no doubt each county would soon, in its turn, provide for itself a sufficiently accurate county map, so that in the course of a very few years a reliable map of the whole territory of the State would be completed.

Such a map should be on a scale of one mile to the inch, for the space thus afforded is not more than sufficient for the multiplicity of names in a densely populated country, a condition that Pennsylvania is approaching. To this may be added a custom of our country—the substitution of new names for old ones —which, even when unadvisable to be retained, should at least be preserved, for the knowledge of that which has been, as well as of that which is, should be easily accessible to all the people of the State. It ought to be that they should be able to find in every school-house such a map as is aimed at, one that—while physically correct—should be truly historical in its character, bearing upon it every name that has ever been applied to a place either by the Indians, the Swedes, the Dutch, the English, or by ourselves; the name of every fort, and site of every battle, the location of the various tribes of Indians, and the paths of their intercourse, the boundaries of purchase under the various treaties, the routes of the armies of Braddock, Armstrong, Forbes, and Bouquet, of Sullivan and Wayne, Howe and Washington, of Lee and Mifflin, and of Lee and Meade, the dates of important events, and the places of birth of men whose arms or inventions, or whose virtues, have added lustre to the State they served.

The Society has received great aid in this work from Messrs. J. Simpson, Africa, Wm. J. Buck, Luke W. Broadhead, Spencer Bonsall, Benjamin Chambers, Harmon A Chambers, Alfred Creigh, the Rev. Leighton Coleman, S. L. Carpenter, John Clement, the Rev. David Craft, Wm. M. Darlington, David Derrickson, Wm. Evans, Wm. H. Egle, M.D., Samuel Evans, J. Smith Futhey, H. J. Fore, A. J Glossbrenner, James L. Gwinn, A. Boyd Hamilton, Fred. Huidekoper, A. C. Haverstick, William A. Irvine, M.D., Samuel D. Irwin, Stueben Jenkins, Robert L. Johnson, John W. Jordan, Strickland Kneass, D. R. Kaine, Thomas King, De B. Randolph Keim, Thomas L. Kane, John B. Linn, the Linnæan Institute, Horace Little, Samuel W. Mifflin, John Hill Martin, David Mahon, M.D., Rev. Joseph A. Murray, D.D., J. L Meredith, Joseph J. Mickley, G. F. Mason, R. A. McCoy, Robert McKim, Peter M. Osterhout, Samuel W. Pennypacker, and the Rev. Wm. C. Reichel.

Historical information on the subjects connected with this map herewith issued, is earnestly desired. It is believed that the Indian names of many streams may yet be rescued, as also a knowledge of the sites of numerous Indian villages.

Communications should be addressed to the Historical Society of Pennsylvania, No. 820 Spruce St., Philadelphia.

TOWNSEND WARD,
Secretary.

HISTORICAL TABLES

Indian Records engraved on Rocks in the Susquehanna
and the Allegheny Rivers, see margin of map
The South or Delaware Bay discovered by Capt. Henry
    Hudson,   1609
Capt. Hendrickson, in the yacht Restless, explores the
    Delaware as far as the Schuylkill,   1616
Capt May gives his name to the Cape,   1618
The Dutch erect Fort Nassau, and make settlements on
    the Delaware,   1623
The Dutch build a trading-house on Biles Island, Bucks
    County,   1626–1627
The Dutch settle at Cape May,   1630
Two ships with Dutch colonists arrive with Capt. De
    Vries,   1631
War between the Lenni Lenapi and the Susquehan-
    nocks,   about 1635
Settlements made by the Swedes under Queen Christina, 1638
Governor Printz settles on Tinicum Island,   1643
Mill erected on Cobb's Creek,   1643
Catechism translated by the Swedes into the Indian lan-
    guage; church built at Tinicum,   1646
Grant to Sir Edmund Ployden, of New Albion, as Gover-
    nor and Earl Palatine,   1648
Upland founded,   1648
Conquest of the Swedes by the Dutch under Peter Stuy-
    vesant,   1655
The Dutch settle at the Minisinks, as traditionally stated,
    prior to   1664

Conquest of the Dutch by the English, under Sir Robert Carr,	1664
George Fox's visit, 1673; Friends Meeting at Upland,	1675
Burlington settled,	1677
First vessel launched on Lake Erie,	1679
William Penn's petition to Charles II. for a grant of territory,	1680
Re-conquest by the Dutch, 1672, Restoration to England 1674, Government by the Duke of York till	1681
The Court under James, Duke of York, sat at Kingsessing,	1681
Grant of the Province to William Penn as Proprietor and Governor, on condition of yielding two beaver skins annually, March 4th,	1681
Penn's arrival; "The Great Law" at Chester; Treaty of Amity under the Elm at Shackamaxon,	1682
William Penn visits King Tamany at Perkasie,	1683
First book printed in the Middle Colonies by William Bradford, at Philadelphia,	1685
First proposal in America to print the Bible, "the first of the first month,"	1687
The liberty of the press first asserted on the earth, by William Bradford on his trial in Philadelphia,	1689
Penn deprived of his authority, 1692, Restored, 30th of August,	1694
Christ Church originally founded,	1695
Paper-mill built by William Bradford and the Rittenhuysens, on the Wissahickon,	1697
Shawanese Indians from Carolina settled on the Susquehanna,	1698
James Logan came to Pennsylvania,	1699
Penn's second visit to the Province, August, 1699; He remained till November,	1701
Philadelphia chartered as a city,	1701
Separation of the Three Lower Counties,	1703

French Huguenots settle on Pequea Creek,	1710
Conrad Weiser came to this country from Germany,	1714
William Penn died at Ruscombe, England, at the age of 74 years, 30th July,	1718
Hannah Penn exercises the Proprietor's prerogatives through representatives, for several years to	1718
First iron made, 1717; The "American Weekly Mercury," published by Andrew Bradford,	1719
Scotch and Irish settlements made in Donegal and Paxton,	1722
First issue of paper-money; Franklin came to Philadelphia,	1723
Log College in Bucks County, founded by Rev. Wm. Tennent,	1726
The Carpenter's Society established, 1724, Bartram's Botanic Garden commenced,	1728
Thomas Godfrey invented the Quadrant,	1730
The Library Company of Philadelphia founded,	1731
"The Colony in Schuylkill," now "The Schuylkill Fishing Company of the State in Schuylkill," founded,	1732
State House commenced, 1729, completed, 1734, Thos Penn resides here, 1732 to 1741, John Penn, 1734 to	1735
Edward Marshall, and others, walked out the purchase of Aug 20, 1686, on the 19th and 20th of September,	1737
Conrad Weiser and William Parsons visit Wyoming,	1738
Christopher Saur, at Germantown, prints the first German Bible in America,	1743
Benjamin West, Artist, born in Delaware County,	1738
First Sunday-school in America commenced at Ephrata,	1740
Whitfield House, at Nazareth, erected,	1740
Sister's House, at Bethlehem, erected,	1743
Lindley Murray, Author, born in Lancaster County,	1745
General Anthony Wayne born, in Chester County,	1745

The Six Nations sell to Geo Croghan 100,000 acres (Allegheny County),	1749
Lewis Evans published a map of the Middle Colonies,	1749
St Andrew's Society [Benevolent] established,	1749
The Loganian Library founded,	1751
Franklin and Kinnersley establish the identity of electricity and lightning,	1752
First Fire Insurance Company in the Colonies, "The Philadelphia Contributionship," established,	1752
Washington's Expedition to Venango, The Forks of the Ohio fortified by his advice, He visits the Half King Tarracharison, and also Queen Alliquippa,	1753
Two expeditions fitted out by Philadelphia Merchants, in search of the Northwest Passage,	1753, 1754
French and Indian War, in which the Western and Central Portions of Pennsylvania were devastated and many of the inhabitants massacred,	1753 to 1763
The French build forts at Presque Isle and Le Bœuf, in April,	1753
Ensign Ward driven from the forks of the Ohio; Fort Du Quesne built, Jumonville defeated; Battle of the Great Meadows; Surrender of Fort Necessity,	1754
David Rittenhouse constructs his Orrery; Pennsylvania Hospital founded; General Braddock defeated, 9th July,	1755
College, Academy, and Charity Schools (now the University of Pennsylvania) founded,	1755
First stage coaches from Philadelphia to New York, and Baltimore,	1756
Gen Armstrong's expedition to Kittaning,	1756
The French retreat from Fort Du Quesne, November 24,	1758
Red Stone Old Fort erected,	1759
A map of the Province published by Nicholas Scull,	1759
Company for Insurance on Lives (Presbyterian) established,	1759

Products of Pennsylvania so vast as to require 8000 to 9000 wagons for transportation to Philadelphia,	1760
Connecticut Settlers arrive at Wyoming, and are attacked by Indians,	1762
Battle of Bushy Run by Col. Bouquet, in the Manor of Denmark,	1763
Pontiac's war,	1763, 1764
Col. Henry Bouquet's expedition against the Indians; Medical School established first in the Colonies,	1764
Robert Fulton born in Lancaster County,	1765
Anthracite coal from Wyoming Valley sent to England (its existence known twenty years previous),	1766
Zeisberger preaches to the Indians at Tionesta, on the 16th October,	1767
Mason and Dixon's Line run,	1763, 1768
American Philosophical Society founded,	1769
Charles Brockden Brown, Novelist, born,	1771
Wilkes-Barré named in honor of John Wilkes and Col Barré,	1773
First steamboat floated on the Schuylkill by Oliver Evans,	1773
Tea destroyed on the Cohansey,	1774
Dispute with Lord Dunmore as to the boundary of Virginia,	1774
First Continental Congress meets in Carpenter's Hall, Sept 5th,	1774
First Troop Philadelphia City Cavalry formed 17th Nov,	1774
Gen Jacob Brown born in Bucks County, May 9th,	1775
Second Continental Congress meets May 10th, and on the 15th of June appoints Washington Commander-in-Chief,	1775
Battles of the Galleys with the British vessels Roebuck and Liverpool, May,	1776
Independence declared in the State House July the 4th,	1776

The Declaration publicly read in the State House Yard on the 8th of July,	1776
Constitution of Pennsylvania signed Sept 28th,	1776
Battle of Trenton, December 26th,	1776
Battle of Princeton, January 3d,	1777
Battle of Brandywine, Sept 11th; Surprise at Paoli, Sept. 20th; Battle of Germantown, October 4th,	1777
Congress removed to Lancaster, Sept. 27th, and to York, Sept 30th, where it sat about nine months,	1777
Capture of Fort Mifflin by the British, Nov. 16,	1777
The British occupy Philadelphia, Sept 26th, 1777, Evacuate it, June 18th,	1778
Battle of Monmouth C H, June 28th,	1778
Frigate Randolph, Capt. Nicholas Biddle, blown up by the Yarmouth off Charleston harbor,	1778
First chartered bank in America (Bank of North America); Wyoming massacre; Gen McIntosh's expedition,	1778
American army at Valley Forge from Dec. 19th, 1777, to June 18th,	1778
Gen Sullivan's expedition up the Susquehanna,	1779
The Royal Charter annulled, and the Penns granted £130,000 sterling for their unseated lands by the Act of November 27th,	1779
The last delivery of two beaver skins at Windsor Castle, by the Proprietaries, for the Province of Pennsylvania, the first of January,	1780
Act abolishing slavery in Pennsylvania; Gen. Brodhead's expedition,	1780
Action between the Hyder Ali and the General Monk, Bucks County riflemen serving as marines,	1782
Robert Aitken, at Philadelphia, prints the first Bible in English in this country,	1782
Albert Gallatin purchases land on the Monongahela, and subsequently establishes glass-works,	1785

The Philadelphia Agricultural Society, the first in the United States, founded July 4th,	1785
Convention to frame the Constitution of the United States sat in Philadelphia,	1787
Revised Constitution of the State,	1790
First steamboat built by John Fitch, 1787; Made regular trips on the Delaware,	1790
Philadelphia the seat of the Federal Government,	1790
Gen. Harmar's expedition against the Miami Indians,	1790
Gen St Clair's expedition, 1792; United States Mint established; commenced coining,	1793
Washington inaugurated President, in Philadelphia, March 4,	1793
Western, or Whisky Insurrection,	1794
Gen. Wayne's Campaign,	1793 to 1795
John Adams inaugurated President, March 4,	1797
Fries' Insurrection,	1798, 1799
Seat of the Federal Government removed from Philadelphia to Washington,	1800
The frigate Philadelphia gallantly burned by Decatur in the Harbor of Tripoli,	1804
Pennsylvania Academy of the Fine Arts founded,	1805
First railroad in the United States, in Delaware County,	1806
Alexander Wilson commences the publication of his "American Ornithology,"	1808
Seat of Government of the State removed to Lancaster, 1799, to Harrisburg,	1812
Academy of Natural Sciences founded,	1812
Washington Benevolent Society of Pennsylvania founded	1812
Perry's fleet built at Erie in seventy days; His victory, September 10th,	1813
The American Flotilla, under Lieut. Angus, engage the British vessel Junon, 38 guns, and Martin 16 guns, outside Crows' shoals, 29 July,	1813

First Light-house on the Great Lakes erected at Presque Isle,	1818
The Franklin Institute founded,	1824
The Historical Society of Pennsylvania founded, Dec. 2d,	1824
Paper made from straw at Meadville, by Col. William Magraw,	1827
Railroad and canal opened to Pittsburgh; Common school system established,	1834
The revised Constitution of the State,	1838
Telegraph lines erected in Pennsylvania,	1846
Pennsylvania Railroad opened to Pittsburgh,	1854
Success of Col. Drake in boring for petroleum, Aug. 29,	1859
Battle of Gettysburg, July,	1863
The revised Constitution of the State,	1874
Centennial of the Independence of the States, International Exposition at Philadelphia, July 4,	1876

All Indian title to territory in Pennsylvania, except the reservation of one mile square on the Allegheny River, has been extinguished by the six treaties mentioned in the table on the Map, and by the purchases of July 15th, 1682, June 23d, 1683, June 25th, 1683; July 14th, 1683, Sept 10th, 1683; Oct 18th, 1683; June 3d, 1684, June 7th, 1684; July 30th, 1685, October 2d, 1685; August 20th, 1686; July 5th, 1691. June 15th, 1692; Sept 13th, 1700 As there were settlements along the River Delaware by the Swedes, the Dutch, and the English under the Duke of York, there was a consequent partial extinguishment of Indian title prior to the grant to William Penn Under Queen Christina, and by her direction, the Indian title to land was extinguished by treaty and purchase.

LIST OF FORTS, BLOCK-HOUSES, AND STOCKADES.

Name.	Date.	Location, etc.
ALLEN,	1756.	Opposite Gnadenhutten, now Weissport, Carbon Co. By Gov. Morris.
ARMSTRONG,	1764.	Franklin.
"	1779.	Armstrong. By order of Gen. Brodhead.
AUGUSTA,	1754.	Shamokin, now Sunbury, Northumberland. By Gov. Morris.
ANDERSON,	1778.	Huntingdon.
ALLEMAENGAL,	1756.	Berks.
ANTES,	1776.	Clinton.
BINGHAM,	1749.	Juniata. By Samuel Bingham.
BEVORSREDE,	1633.	Near the mouth of Schuylkill. By the Dutch.
BETHLEHEM,	1756.	Stockaded in part.
BEDFORD,	1763.	Bedford.
BURD,	1759.	Site of Redstone Old Fort, Brownsville, Fayette.
BRADY,	1777.	On Muncy Creek, Lycoming.
BRODHEAD,	1755.	A block-house, Monroe.
BILLINGSPORT,	1776.	Gloucester, N. J. By Committee of Safety of Pennsylvania.
BROWN,	1756.	On the Swatara, Dauphin.
"	1778.	Pittston, Luzerne.
CROGHAN,	1754.	A trading-house, Cumberland.
CUMBERLAND,	1754.	On Wills' Creek, Cumberland Co., Md. By Col. James Innes, of Va.

Name	Date	Location, etc
CRAWFORD,	1779.	Westmoreland. By Col Wm Crawford.
CHRISTINA,	1638.	Near Wilmington, Delaware By the Swedes.
CHAMBERS,	1756	Chambersburg, Franklin. By Benjamin Chambers.
CASIMIR,	1651.	New Castle, Delaware. By the Dutch.
DU QUESNE,	1754.	Pittsburgh, Allegheny By the French.
DIETZ,	1756	One mile south of Wind Gap, Northampton Co. A Stockade
DICKEY,	1764	Cumberland.
DEPUI,	1755.	On the Delaware, Monroe A stockade. By Samuel Depui
DAVIS,	1756.	Franklin. By Philip Davis
DURKEE,	1769.	Wilkes-Barré, Luzerne. By the Connecticut settlers.
ELSINGBURG,	1643.	Salem Co., N. J. By the Swedes.
EVERETT,	1756.	Lynn Tp., Lehigh. By John Everett.
ERIE,	1795	Erie. Three block-houses built.
"	1813.	Erie Two block-houses built.
FERGUSON,	1764	Cumberland.
FREELAND,	1773.	Northumberland.
FREDERICK,	1756.	On the Potomac, Md.
FORTY,	1770.	Kingston, Luzerne. By the Wyoming settlers.
FROMAN,	1755.	Washington
FUTTER	1777.	Blan.
FRANKLIN,	1756	Schuylkill.
"		At Shippensburg, Cumberland
"	1787.	Venango. By U. S troops

Name.	Date.	Location, etc.
FRIEDENSTHAL,	1756.	Two miles N. E. from Nazareth, Northampton. A stockade.
GNADENTHAL,	1756.	One mile W. of Nazareth. Stockaded.
GRANVILLE,	1755.	Near Lewistown, Mifflin.
HAMILTON,	1755.	Stroudsburgh, Monroe.
HAND,	1778.	Westmoreland.
HALIFAX,	1756.	Dauphin. By Col. Wm. Clapham.
HARRIS,	1756.	Harrisburg, Dauphin. A stockade. By John Harris.
HENRY,	1754.	Lebanon. Also called Swatara, or Capt. Busse's Fort. By Gov. Morris.
HUNTER,	1755.	Dauphin.
HYNDSHAW,	1756.	Monroe.
JENKINS,	1776.	One mile above Fort Wintermoot, Luzerne.
"	1777.	Near Centreville, Columbia.
LEBANON,	1754.	On the Bohundy Creek, Schuylkill. Also called Fort William.
LE BŒUF,	1753.	Near Waterford, Erie. By the French.
LEHIGH GAP,	1756.	Northampton. A stockade.
LE TORT,	1753.	Near Carlisle, Cumberland. A trading-house.
LIGONIER,	1757.	Westmoreland Co.
LOWRY,	1779.	Blair.
LOWTHER,	1753.	Carlisle, Cumberland.
LOUDOUN,	1756.	Franklin. By Col. John Armstrong.
LYTTLETON,	1756.	Fulton. By Gov. Morris.
MANADY,	1755.	Dauphin.
MCALEVEY,		Huntingdon.
MCALLISTER,	1764.	Cumberland.

Name	Date	Location, etc.
McClure,	1781	Columbia.
McConnel,	1764.	Franklin.
McCord,	1756.	Franklin
McDowell,	1756.	Franklin. At McDowell's Mill.
McIntosh,	1778	Beaver. By Gen McIntosh
McKee,	1756.	Northumberland. By Capt. Thos. McKee.
Mercer,	1777	Gloucester, N. J. Opposite Fort Mifflin.
Mifflin,	1774.	Below the mouth of Schuylkill. Called also Mud Fort.
Miller,		Washington A block-house
"	1782.	Westmoreland.
Montgomery,	1779	Montour.
Morris,	1755.	Shippensburg, Cumberland.
Muncy,	1778.	Lycoming. By Col. Thomas Hartley Sometimes called Wallis.
Nassau,	1623	Gloucester, N J By the Dutch.
Nazareth,	1756	Northampton. Stockaded
Necessity,	1754.	Fayette By Major Washington.
New Gottenburg,	1643	On Tinicum Island, Delaware Co., By the Swedes
Norris,	1756.	Monroe.
Northkill,	1754.	Berks.
Ogden,	1769.	A block-house near Wilkes-Barré. Luzerne.
Oplandt,	1631.	Lewes, Delaware. By the Dutch.
Patterson,	1751.	Snyder.
Penn,	1763	Stroudsburg, Monroe In place of Fort Hamilton
Pitt,	1758.	Pittsburgh, on the site of Fort Du Quesne. By Col. Mercer
Pitiston,	1776.	Luzerne. A stockade

Name.	Date.	Location, etc.
POMFRET CASTLE,	1756.	On Mahantango Creek, Snyder. By Gov. Morris.
POTTER,	1768.	Penn's Valley, Centre.
PRESQUE ISLE,	1753.	Erie. By the French.
REED,	1778.	Lock Haven, Clinton.
"	1782.	Westmoreland.
RED BANK,	1777.	Gloucester, N. J.
REDSTONE OLD FORT,	1759.	Brownsville, Fayette.
RICE,	1774.	Washington.
"	1780.	Near Washingtonville, Montour.
ROBERDEAU,	1778.	Sinking Spring Valley, Blair. Also called Lead Mine Fort.
SCHWARTZ,	1780.	One mile above Milton, Northumberland.
SHIRLEY,	1755.	Huntingdon. By Gov. Morris.
STANDING STONE,	1762.	Huntingdon.
STEELE,	1755.	Three miles east of Mercersburg, Franklin.
SWATARA,	1757.	Lebanon. Also called Fort Henry.
TIOGA POINT,	1779.	Bradford. A stockade. By Gen. Sullivan.
VENANGO,	1754.	Venango. By the French. Sometimes called Fort Machault.
WALLACE,	1778.	Westmoreland.
WINTERMOOT,	1777.	Luzerne. By the Wyoming settlers.
WOLF,		Washington. By Jacob Wolf.
WYOMING,	1771.	Luzerne.

MANORS.

THE DATES OF THOSE MARKED* ARE OF THE RE-SURVEY.

Manors	To whom granted	Date	Acres	Location and remarks
AMORLAND OR BILTON	Wm and Marg Lowther	1733	2,850	Chester Co
AMSTERDAM ROTTERDAM	Proprietaries	1768	2,770	Northumberland, now Luzerne—"at Nescopeck"
ANTOLHOUGH OR ANDOLHEA	Richard Penn	1741	5,000	Lancaster—[probably the same as "Little Swatara Manor"]
BEDFORD FORT	Proprietaries	1762	2,810	Bedford—"including the town of Bedford—a Royal Draft"
BILTON	John Penn	1701	9,810	Chester
CALLOWHILL	Thos Callowhill	1702	5,000	Chester—"on a branch of French Creek"
FELL	Charles Fell and Guhelma Maria Fell	1727	10,000	Lancaster—"on Tulpehocken Creek"
CHAWTON	John Page	1735	1,500	Northampton Co—' on a branch of the Hockendocqua "
CHERRY HILL	Proprietaries	1763	1,202	Westmoreland, now Indiana—"on the waters of Twolick on the path leading from Frankstown to Kittanning"
CHEST	"	1763	1,123	Bedford, now Cambria [?]—' on the heads of the waters of the Chest and Clearfield Creek, about two miles west from the Great Clearfield "
CONESTOGA	William Penn	1717	16,000	Lancaster
DENMARK	Proprietaries	1769	4,861	Westmoreland—"at Bushey Run"
DUNDEE	"	1773	3,520	Northumberland, now Bradford—"on Wyaloosing Creek"
FAGG (SIR JOHN)	Letitia Aubrey William Penn	*1737	39,250	Chester — "near Marlbrow"
FERMOR	Proprietaries	1736		Northampton—[no record] Or Dry Lands
FREAME	Thomas Freame	1733	2,500	Bucks Co—"in Rockland Township" — "Part of Perkasea Mannom"
FREAME	Thomas Freame	1741	10,000	Lancaster, now Schuylkill,—"on the N E branch of Swatara"
GILBERTS	Proprietaries	*1733	4,095	Philadelphia, now Montgomery
HEMPFIELD	"	1720	2,816	Lancaster.
HIGHLAND	"	1755	7,750	Bucks

Manors	To whom granted	Date	Acres	Location and remarks
HIGHLANDS	Proprietaries	1767	763	Bedford, *now Blair* — "in the Warrior's Valley, on the N W. side of Warrior Ridge and S E side of Tussy's Mt "
INDIAN LANDING	"	1773	1,866	Northumberland, *now Bradford*— 'on the south side of N E branch of Susquehanna opposite the mouth of Owegy "
INDIAN TRACT	"	1767	6,300	Northampton — "in the Forks of Delaware "
KITTANING	"	1770	3,960	Westmoreland, *now Armstrong*
LECHAWAXSIN } LACKAWAXIN }	"	1748	12,150	Northampton, *now Pike*
LETITIA AUBREYS	Letitia Aubrey	*1737	5,000	Chester—"on Elk River "
LITTLE SWATARA	Richard Penn	1741	5,000	Lancaster, *now Schuylkill* —"on Little Swatara "
LOWTHER	Proprietaries	1767	7,557	Cumberland — [once called Paxton Manor]
MASKE	Thos and Rich Penn	1741	43,500	York, *now Adams*
MACUNGY	Proprietaries	1762	5,000	Northampton, *now Lehigh*— " Barrens of Macungie "
MANATAWNY	John Penn	1701	12,000	Philadelphia, *now Montgomery*
MORELAND	Nicholas More	1684	9,815	Philadelphia, *now chiefly in Montgomery*
MOUNT JOY	Letitia Penn	1683	5,000	Philadelphia, *now Montgomery*
MUNCY	Proprietaries	1768	1,802	Northumberland, *now Lycoming*
NOTTINGHAM	"	1770	1,035	Westmoreland, *now Washington*
PAXTANG	Thomas Penn	1732	1,272	Dauphin—on Susquehanna and Paxtang Creek, "adjoining John Harris' land "
PENNS	Wm Penn, Jr	1704	5,000	Chester—"adjoining Fagg's Manor "
PINE GROVE	Proprietaries	1773	4,545	Northumberland, *now Bradford*—"on the S E side of the N E branch of Susquehanna, adjoining the above " [St. David's]
PENNSBURY	Wm Penn	1683	8,431	Bucks
PENN's LODGE	Proprietaries	1769	5,568	Westmoreland — "on Sewickley, about fourteen miles from Legonier "
PERKASIE } PERKISSEY }	Richard Penn	*1735	11,462	Bucks
PITTSBURG	Proprietaries	1769	5,766	Westmoreland *now Allegheny*—"to include Pittsburgh "
POMFRET	"	1768	4,766	Northumberland—"at Shamokin. '

Manors	To whom granted	Date	Acres	Location and remarks
RICHLAND	Wm Penn	1703	16,749	Bucks — "in the Great Swamp" Probably Buck Township, Luzerne Co,
ROTERDAM (see AMSTERDAM)				called "the Shades of Death"
RUSCOMBE	Proprietaries	1739	10,000	Berks—"near Oley"
ST DAVID'S	"	1773	3,002	Northumberland, *now Bradford*—"on the east side of the N E branch of Susquehanna River, beginning about two miles below Owegy and extending along the river, &ca"
SEWICKLEY	Proprietaries	1769	5,568	Westmoreland—also called Penn's Lodge
SHARON	Henry Montour	1761	1,710	Cumberland, *now Mifflin*—"in Kishacoquillas Valley"
SHAVER'S CREEK	Proprietaries	1763	2,571	Bedford, *now Huntingdon*
SINKING VALLEY	"	1763	9,056	Bedford, *now Blair*
SPRINGEFTSLURY	Wm Penn	*1703	1,840	Philadelphia
SPRINGETTSBURY	Springett Penn	1722	64,520	York
SPRINGFIELD	Gulielma Maria Penn	1687	4,010	Philadelphia, *now Montgomery*—"on a branch of Schuylkill"
SPRINGTOWN SPRINGTON	Wm Penn	1701	10,000	Chester.
STOKE	Proprietaries	1769	9,800	Northumberland, *now Luzerne*—"opposite the Manor of Sunbury" This is now the City of Wilkes-Barré
SUNBURY	"	1769	20,000	Northumberland, *now Luzerne*—"on the N W side of the N E branch of Susquehanna at Wyoming," now the town of Plymouth
TULPEHOCKEN	Richard Penn	1765	7,510	Berks
VINCENT	Vincent, Cox, and Thompson	1686	30,000	Chester — "west side of Schuylkill about Turkey Point"
WALLENPAUPACK	Proprietaries	1748	12,150	Bucks, *now Wayne*—"at Lehighwaxscet" At or near the village of Hawley
WAPHALLOPEN	"	1768	601	Northumberland, *now Luzerne*—"on Wappallopen Creek and Susquehanna River, Hollenback township"
		1683 1704		
WM PENN	Wm Penn		5,000	Chester
WILLIAMSTADT	Wm Penn, Jr.	1773	7,482	Philadelphia, *now Montgomery*
WYOMING	Proprietaries		10,000	Northumberland, *now Bradford*—"from below Wyaloosing to Towanda Creek and Owegy"
YORKTOWN	"		421	York [part of Springettsbury]

In addition to those in the foregoing list, warrants were issued for the following Lands for the Proprietaries, and were to all intents and purposes Manors, and should be so classed, although they are not among the Records of the Land Department of Pennsylvania.

SAFE HARBOR, 1773.		2,222.	West side of Delaware River, at the mouth of Equinunk Creek.
DAMASCUS,	"	4,390.	Northampton County, at Coshictung, on Delaware and Cashe's Creek.
		2,770.	Northampton Co., on Lackawaxen Creek.
WILLIAM PENN, JR.,		5,214.	Wayne County, on Lackawaxen and Equinunk Creeks.
THE MEADOWS,	1763.	3,032.	East side of Moosic, on waters of Lackawaxen Creek.
THE MILL SEAT,	"	999.	On most southerly branch of Equinunk, or 5½ miles from Delaware.
DUCK'S HARBOR,	"	510.	Head waters Little Equinunk Creek, 5 miles from Delaware.
FOX HARBOR,	"	1,694.	East branch of Lackawaxen.
BEAVER HARBOR,	"	665.	On Beaver pond, branch of Quacake Creek, 100 perches west of Nescopeck Creek.
COW-PASTURE,	"	3,603.	On most westerly Creek, Tamaqua or L. Schuylkill.
PLEASANT GARDEN,	"	20,948.	On Big Middle Creek, a westerly creek of Leckawaxin.
SANDY RUN,	"	1,280.	East branch of Lackawaxen, called Sandy Run, 10 miles from Delaware.
TERRAPIN HARBOR,	"	839.	On Terrapin Creek, north side Broad Mountain, on path from Gnadenhutten to Wyoming.
BREWER'S DEN,	"	312.	On a branch of Equinunk Creek.
SHOHOCKING,	"	520.	On west side of Delaware, at mouth of Popactunk.
ELK FOREST,	"	11,526.	On waters of Lackawaxen and Big Middle Creek.
		12,300.	Between Ruscombe Manor and Reading.
CROOKED DALE, 1769.		1,026.	Northumberland County. N. E. branch of Susquehanna River.

Job's Discovery,	1,615	On west branch Susquehanna River, at mouth of Muncy
	2,473	In Warrior Valley, N W side of Ridge and S E side of Cove Mountain
	1,497	Two miles above Frankstown
	463	On head of Water Street.
Lake Paupunauming,	215	Hamilton Township, Monroe Co Lake 190 poles long
Vineyard,	2,000	On Andalusia Creek, 60 miles from Phila
Jerico on Delaware,	596	In Mount Bethel Township, Northampton County
	994	On east side of Susquehanna, in Columbia and Luzerne Counties

MANORS

IN THE THREE LOWER COUNTILS

Duke of York,	James, Duke of York,	1683, 10,000	Sussex	On the Rich Ridge
Frieth,	William Penn	1683, 10,240	Kent	"At Duck Creek"
Rockland,	William Penn.	1683.	New Castle	
———	"	1683, 17,100	Sussex	On Nanticoke River
———	"	1683, 4,790	Sussex	On Cedar Creek

PUBLICATION FUND

OF THE

HISTORICAL SOCIETY OF PENNSYLVANIA.

820 SPRUCE STREET, PHILADELPHIA

HALL OPEN FROM 10 A M TO 10 P M

A subscription of twenty-five dollars to this Fund obtains the right to receive during life a copy of each work issued. For libraries, a subscription secures the right for twenty years. The money received is placed in securities held by the Trustees, who use only the accruing interest. More than nine hundred persons and libraries, in nineteen different States, and in Canada, Cuba, England, France, Germany, and Italy, have thus far subscribed It is desirable, however, that the number should be very largely increased, in order to secure a more speedy issue of valuable works.

Payments may be made at any time at the Hall of the Society, or by check or post-office order, made payable to the order of JOHN JORDAN, Jr.

TOWNSEND WARD,

JULY, 1873 *Secretary*

TRUSTEES	PRESENT STATE OF
JOHN JORDAN, JR ,	FUND,
AUBREY II SMITH,	INTEREST ONLY USED
FAIRMAN ROGERS	$22,000

WORKS ALREADY PUBLISHED

History of Braddock's Expedition.
Contributions to American History, 1858
Record of Upland, and Denny's Military Journal
Republication of Memoirs of the Society, Vol I
Minutes of the Committee of Defence of Philadelphia
Penn and Logan Correspondence, Vol I.
Penn and Logan Correspondence, Vol II
Acrelius's New Sweden. Translated by REYNOLDS
Historical Map of Pennsylvania